W9-BNQ-817

DISASTER ZONE
SINKHOLES

by Vanessa Black

pogo

Ideas for Parents and Teachers

Pogo Books let children practice reading informational text while introducing them to nonfiction features such as headings, labels, sidebars, maps, and diagrams, as well as a table of contents, glossary, and index.

Carefully leveled text with a strong photo match offers early fluent readers the support they need to succeed.

Before Reading

- "Walk" through the book and point out the various nonfiction features. Ask the student what purpose each feature serves.

- Look at the glossary together. Read and discuss the words.

Read the Book

- Have the child read the book independently.

- Invite him or her to list questions that arise from reading.

After Reading

- Discuss the child's questions. Talk about how he or she might find answers to those questions.

- Prompt the child to think more. Ask: Have you ever been somewhere a sinkhole might occur?

Pogo Books are published by Jump!
5357 Penn Avenue South
Minneapolis, MN 55419
www.jumplibrary.com

Library of Congress Cataloging-in-Publication Data

Names: Black, Vanessa.
Title: Sinkholes / by Vanessa Black.
Description: Minneapolis, MN: Jump!, Inc., 2016.
Series: Disaster zone Audience: Age 7-10. Includes index.
Identifiers: LCCN 2016029501 (print)
LCCN 2016030431 (ebook)
ISBN 9781620315651 (hard cover: alk. paper)
ISBN 9781620316054 (pbk.)
ISBN 9781624965135 (e-book)
Subjects: LCSH: Sinkholes–Juvenile literature.
Classification: LCC GB609.2 .B53 2016 (print)
LCC GB609.2 (ebook) | DDC 551.44/7–dc23
LC record available at https://lccn.loc.gov/2016029501

Editor: Kirsten Chang
Series Designer: Anna Peterson
Book Designer: Leah Sanders
Photo Researchers: Kirsten Chang and Leah Sanders

Photo Credits: Alamy, 3, 4, 5; AP Images, 6-7, 8-9, 10-11, 17, 18-19; Getty, cover, 14-15, 16, 20-21; Shutterstock, 1, 12-13, 16, 23.

Printed in the United States of America at Corporate Graphics in North Mankato, Minnesota.

TABLE OF CONTENTS

CHAPTER 1

IT'S A SINKHOLE!

Imagine you are in Florida. Up the road, you see a house. It tilts. The ground buckles.

Watch out! A big hole in the ground opens. The house falls in. It's a sinkhole!

Sinkholes are holes in the ground. They form when water **erodes** rocks and minerals underground. Eventually, the underground structure cannot hold up the earth's surface. The surface collapses.

DID YOU KNOW?

Sinkholes are also called sinks, swallows, and dolines.

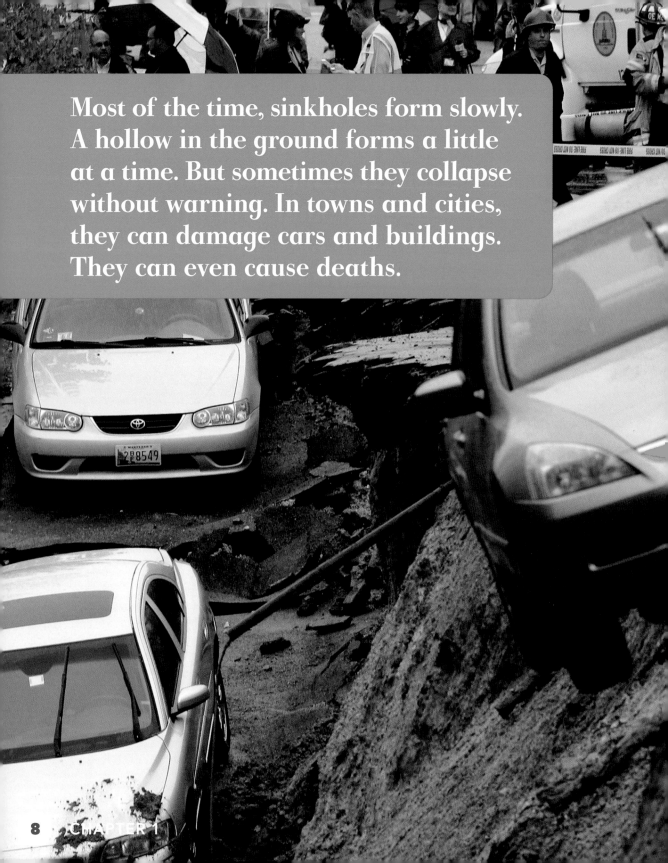

Most of the time, sinkholes form slowly. A hollow in the ground forms a little at a time. But sometimes they collapse without warning. In towns and cities, they can damage cars and buildings. They can even cause deaths.

TAKE A LOOK!

How do sinkholes form in nature?

1 It rains. Rain falls into cracks in the **bedrock**.
2 The rain slowly wears away the rock.
3 Caves form. At this time, the ground above stays intact.
4 It rains more. The caves expand.
5 Soon, there is not enough rock under the surface.
6 The ground falls.

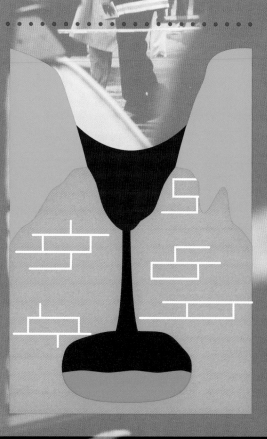

■ = sinkhole
☐ = soil
▨ = limestone bedrock
■ = cave
☐ = water

Humans cause sinkholes, too. **Mining** creates empty areas in the earth. They can collapse.

Or an underground water pipe might burst. It causes rocks to erode. A big space under the ground forms. Eventually the ground cannot stay up. It falls.

DID YOU KNOW?

Sinkholes are usually round.

Sinkholes can happen underwater. The Great Blue Hole is a large ocean sinkhole. It is in **Belize**. It is 984 feet across (300 meters). That's about as long as 10 basketball courts! It is 410 feet (125 m) deep.

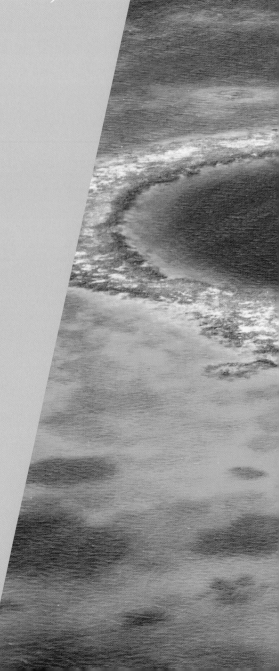

DID YOU KNOW?

You can scuba dive in The Great Blue Hole. It is home to sharks and reef fish.

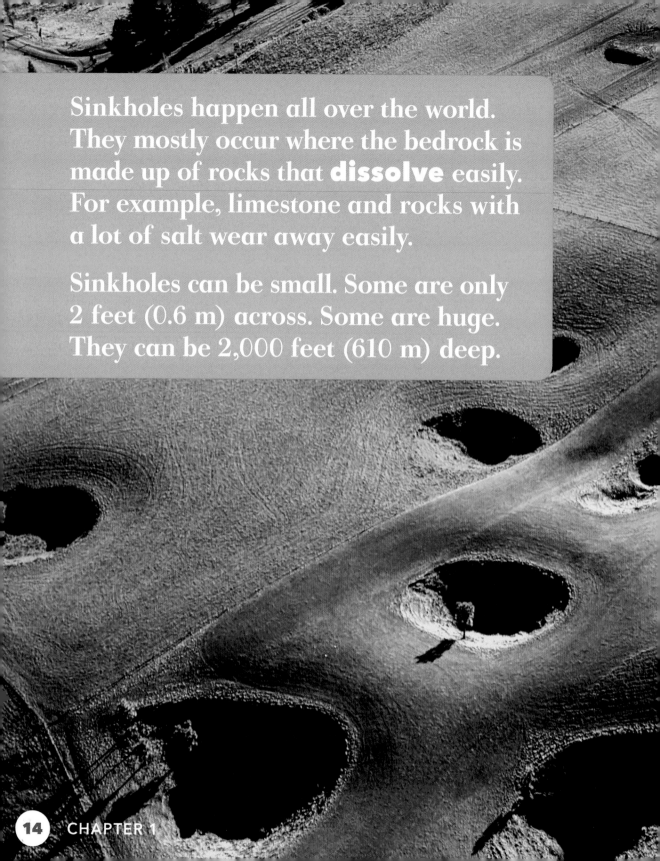

Sinkholes happen all over the world. They mostly occur where the bedrock is made up of rocks that **dissolve** easily. For example, limestone and rocks with a lot of salt wear away easily.

Sinkholes can be small. Some are only 2 feet (0.6 m) across. Some are huge. They can be 2,000 feet (610 m) deep.

WHERE DO THEY HAPPEN?

Sinkholes are more common in areas of **karst terrain.**

UNITED STATES

■ = Karst Terrain Areas

CHAPTER 2

SUDDEN SINKHOLES

In the United States, most reported sinkholes occur in the South. In one example from 2013, Jeff Bush went to sleep in his bed in Florida.

sinkhole

Then the ground opened up. A sinkhole! He called to his brother, but dirt and rocks covered him. He was never found.

In 2007 and 2010, gigantic holes suddenly formed in Guatemala City. They swallowed homes, cars, and people.

They were widely reported as sinkholes. But that was not technically accurate. The ground under true sinkholes is limestone. But the ground under Guatemala City is volcanic ash and rock.

The effect, however, was the same. The 2007 hole killed five people. The 2010 hole swallowed a three-story building.

CHAPTER 3

STAYING SAFE

Sinkholes are hard to **predict**. If you live in an area **prone** to sinkholes, look out for certain things. Trees may sag. Doors or windows may not close. Puddles of water may collect in odd places.

If you see these things, tell an adult. Never go near a sinkhole. The ground may not be **stable**. With help from **engineers** or **geologists**, you may be able to tell if a sinkhole could happen.

ACTIVITIES & TOOLS

MAKE A SINKHOLE

What causes a sinkhole? Explore the physics behind sinkholes in this simple experiment.

What You Need:
- a glass jar
- sugar cubes
- graham crackers
- dirt
- water

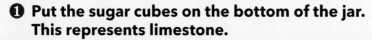

❶ Put the sugar cubes on the bottom of the jar. This represents limestone.

❷ Stack a layer of graham cracker on top of the sugar cubes. This represents soil.

❸ Put a layer of dirt on top of the graham cracker. This represents topsoil.

❹ Slowly, add drops of water to the dirt. This acts as rain.

❺ Note what happens. Do you see a sinkhole?

GLOSSARY

bedrock: Rock that is under the ground.

Belize: A small country in Central America.

dissolve: Come apart in water.

engineers: People who design and build things.

erodes: Wears away, as if by the action of water or wind.

geologists: Scientists that study rocks and the earth.

karst terrain: An area marked by caves and underground channels formed by eroded rock such as limestone.

mining: Removing things from inside the earth (like diamonds or gold) through pits or tunnels.

predict: To make a good guess if something is going to happen.

prone: Likely to do or happen.

stable: Fixed, not moving or changing.

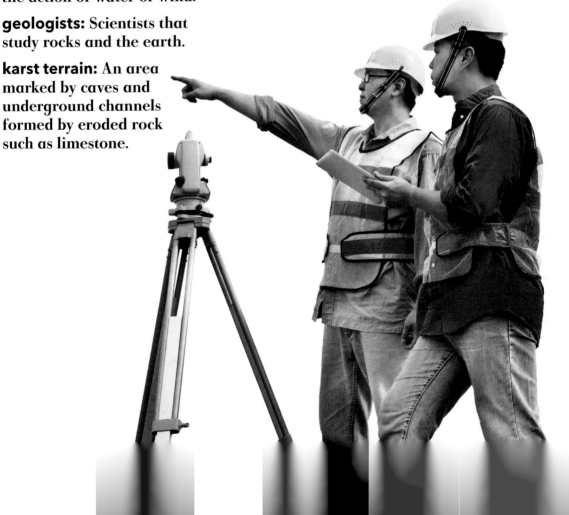

INDEX

TO LEARN MORE

Learning more is as easy as 1, 2, 3.

1) **Go to www.factsurfer.com**

2) **Enter "sinkholes" into the search box.**

3) **Click the "Surf" button to see a list of websites.**

With factsurfer, finding more information is just a click away.